IMAGES OF WAR

HITLER'S DEATH CAMPS IN OCCUPIED POLAND

RARE PHOTOGRAPHS FROM WARTIME ARCHIVES

Ian Baxter

Pen & Sword
MILITARY

First published in Great Britain in 2021 by
PEN & SWORD MILITARY
an imprint of
Pen & Sword Books Ltd
47 Church Street
Barnsley
South Yorkshire
S70 2AS

ISBN 978-1-52676-541-3

A CIP catalogue record for this book is available from the British Library.

Typeset by Concept, Huddersfield, West Yorkshire HD4 5JL
Printed and bound in England by CPI Group (UK) Ltd, Croydon CR0 4YY

Pen & Sword Books Limited incorporates the imprints of Atlas, Archaeology, Aviation, Discovery, Family History, Fiction, History, Maritime, Military, Military Classics, Politics, Select, Transport, True Crime, Air World, Frontline Publishing, Leo Cooper, Remember When, Seaforth Publishing, The Praetorian Press, Wharncliffe Local History, Wharncliffe Transport, Wharncliffe True Crime and White Owl.

For a complete list of Pen & Sword titles please contact
PEN & SWORD BOOKS LIMITED
47 Church Street, Barnsley, South Yorkshire S70 2AS, England
E-mail: enquiries@pen-and-sword.co.uk
Website: www.pen-and-sword.co.uk

Contents

About the Author

Ian Baxter is a military historian who specialises in German twentieth-century military history. He has written more than fifty books including *Poland – The Eighteen Day Victory March*, *Panzers In North Africa*, *The Ardennes Offensive*, *The Western Campaign*, *The 12th SS Panzer-Division Hitlerjugend*, *The Waffen-SS on the Western Front*, *The Waffen-SS on the Eastern Front*, *The Red Army at Stalingrad*, *Elite German Forces of World War II*, *Armoured Warfare*, *German Tanks of War*, *Blitzkrieg*, *Panzer-Divisions at War*, *Hitler's Panzers*, *German Armoured Vehicles of World War Two*, *Last Two Years of the Waffen-SS at War*, *German Soldier Uniforms and Insignia*, *German Guns of the Third Reich*, *Defeat to Retreat: The Last Years of the German Army At War 1943–45*, *Operation Bagration – the Destruction of Army Group Centre*, *German Guns of the Third Reich*, *Rommel and the Afrika Korps*, *U-Boat War*, and most recently *The Sixth Army and the Road to Stalingrad*. He has written over a hundred articles including 'Last days of Hitler', 'Wolf's Lair', 'The Story of the V1 and V2 Rocket Programme', 'Secret Aircraft of World War Two', 'Rommel at Tobruk', 'Hitler's War With his Generals', 'Secret British Plans to Assassinate Hitler', 'The SS at Arnhem', 'Hitlerjugend', 'Battle of Caen 1944', 'Gebirgsjäger at War', 'Panzer Crews', 'Hitlerjugend Guerrillas', 'Last Battles in the East', 'The Battle of Berlin', and many more. He has also reviewed numerous military studies for publication, supplied thousands of photographs and important documents to various publishers and film production companies worldwide, and lectures to various schools, colleges and universities throughout the United Kingdom and the Republic of Ireland.

Chapter One

Prelude to the Final Solution

When the Nazis conquered Poland at the end of September 1939, the Germans acquired territory with a population of 20 million, of whom 17 million were Poles and 675,000 Germans. Before invading, Hitler had already decided that he would clear the Poles and Jews out of the incorporated areas and replace them with German settlers. What followed was a period of unrestrained terror in Poland, particularly in the incorporated territories. The unincorporated areas, consisting of the province of Lublin and parts of the provinces of Warsaw and Krakow, contained a population of 11 million. It was initially termed the 'General Government of the Occupied Polish Areas' and in 1940 was renamed the 'General Government'. It became the dumping ground for all undesirables and those deemed enemies of the state. It was here that the first deportations of Poles and Jews were sent.

In early 1940 the General Government absorbed many thousands of people. Relocating Poles and Jews became an administrative nightmare and it was agreed that the Jews should be forced to live in ghettos. This would not only relieve the burden of the resettlement programme, but it was a way of temporarily getting rid of the 'Jewish problem'. The Nazis propagated the belief that the Eastern Jews in particular were carriers of disease and needed to be isolated.

Meanwhile, the SS pursued harsh policies to deal with the threat of subversion by Polish nationalists and Jewish Bolshevists in the newly incorporated territories. By early 1940 the various detention centres of the Reich had become full to bursting due to the large numbers deemed enemies of the state. News circulated through SS channels that government officials were demanding immediate action in the expansion of the concentration camp system through its new conquered territory, Poland. The German authorities quickly pressed forward to establish camps in Poland where prisoners could be incarcerated and set to work as stonebreakers and construction workers for buildings and streets. It was envisaged that the Poles would remain as a slave labour force, and 'quarantine camps' were established to subdue the local population.

Initially it was proposed that the quarantine camps would hold the prisoners until they were sent to concentration camps in the Reich. But it soon became apparent that this was impractical, and it was approved that these camps were to function as permanent prisons. Throughout 1940 the SS concentration camp system in Poland expanded rapidly.

While the Jews were imprisoned in ghettos, the Germans invaded the Soviet Union and the Jewish problem escalated further as thousands of Jews and other creeds regarded by the Nazis as 'subhuman' entered the area controlled by the Reich.

Although shooting was effective as a method of killing, commanders soon became aware it had disadvantages. Firstly, the killings were difficult to conceal and were often witnessed by unauthorized persons, who often complained at the brutality.

Secondly it was distressing for the killers. Himmler was aware of the problems of mass execution. In August 1941 near Minsk he witnessed a mass killing and nearly fainted. He commented to a commander that the execution was not humane and the effects on the troops would lower morale. Meanwhile he told the army that they would have to accept the liquidations in the East as policy as it was a matter of ideology.

One idea was to get other people to do the killing: Poles, Ukrainians, Balts, and Jews who were anyway going to be killed. This was better, especially when rounding up and killing women and children. But shooting was still not a fast enough way to kill the huge numbers they wanted to kill. Himmler made it clear he required a more effective method, such as explosives or gas.

Gas was not a new method to the Nazis. A special department known as T4 had organized the 'euthanasia programme', which used gas to kill the insane and incurably ill. The programme was a success and run for two years, but due to public opinion it was reluctantly suspended. Now it was proposed that this method of killing should be used outside Germany against enemies of the state in the East, and plans were set in motion.

Gas was introduced for the first time to the killing squads known as Einsatzgruppen. A special airtight vehicle was built to resemble an ambulance. The victims would be placed in the cabin and carbon monoxide pumped in. In the autumn of 1941 the first gas van prepared for the Eastern Front was tested on Russian prisoners of war in Sachsenhausen concentration camp.

Although many thousands of Jews and Russians were captured and murdered in the new gas vans, they were still not popular with the SS. But they were to remain the preferred method of killing for the time being.

Gas vans were also used near the first extermination centre which was built in the Polish village of Chełmno nad Nerem, 31 miles north of Łódź.

(**Opposite**) Two showing the carnage the Nazi wrought on Poland during the invasion of the country in September 1939. By 5 October Poland had surrendered and Hitler was determined to destroy the country politically and racially.

(**Opposite, above**) A Jewish gentleman in the town of Przemyśl on 15 September is being humiliated by a German soldier by cutting some of his beard off. *(ARC)*

(**Opposite, below**) A policeman assists the Germans with rounding up Jewish people and those suspected to be members of the intelligentsia and other political prisoners.

(**Above**) German soldiers are undertaking house-to-house searches in a Polish town. A Jewish boy has been called out from inside his house and runs out to join other Jews.

Jews being rounded up in Lublin on
3 September.

Portrait of Hans Frank, the German
Governor-General of Poland from 1939 to
1945. After the German invasion of Poland
in 1939, Frank was appointed Governor-
General of the occupied Polish territories.
During his appointment, he instituted a
reign of terror against the civilian
population and became directly implicated
in the mass murder of Jews. He was also
responsible for directing orders for the use
of forced labour, deportation, helping in the
planning for the ghetto system, and
oversaw four of the extermination camps.

(**Left**) SS-Obergruppenführer Odilo Globocnik, SS and Police Leader for the Lublin district of Poland in November 1939. In May 1942, SS-Reichsführer Heinrich Himmler put him in charge of Operation Reinhard, the plan for the extermination of Polish Jewry utilizing three death camps: Treblinka, Belzec and Sobibor.

(**Right**) Reinhard Heydrich, a main architect of the Holocaust, chief of the Reich Main Security Office (including the Gestapo, Kripo and SD). He was also deputy Protector of Bohemia and Moravia. Heydrich was instrumental in carrying out plans for the extermination of the Jews in Europe and in the East. It is generally believed that Aktion Reinhard was named after Reinhard Heydrich.

A photo of SS-Reichsführer Heinrich Himmler (right) of the SS, who was one of the most powerful men in Nazi Germany. He was also the main architect of the Holocaust and directed the murder of millions of innocent people due to his extreme racial and political views.

BERLIN, den 1.Sept.1939.

ADOLF HITLER

Reichsleiter B o u h l e r   und

Dr. med. B r a n d t

sind unter Verantwortung beauftragt, die Befug -

nisse namentlich zu bestimmender Ärzte so zu er -

weitern, dass nach menschlichem Ermessen unheilbar

Kranken bei kritischster Beurteilung ihres Krank -

heitszustandes der Gnadentod gewährt werden kann.

[signature]

[handwritten note] Von Bouhler mir
übergeben am 27.8.40
Dr. Gürtner

Io 3/41 gRs/

Copy of a letter signed by Hitler authorizing the T4 (euthanasia) program. It states: 'Reichsleiter [Philipp] Bouhler and Dr. med. [Karl] Brandt are charged with responsibility to broaden the authority of certain doctors to the extent that [persons] suffering from illnesses judged to be incurable may, after a humane, most careful assessment of their condition, be granted a mercy death. [signed] Adolf Hitler.' In 1940, ordered by Himmler, Franz Stangl became superintendent of the T4 Euthanasia Programme at Schloss Hartheim. Here people with mental and physical disabilities, as well as political prisoners, were sent to be killed. *(USHMM)*

SS-Reichsführer Heinrich Himmler of the SS inspects some of his Waffen-SS soldiers. (NARA)

Jewish people being escorted along a road through a town. Following the German invasion of Poland there was a period of unrestrained terror, particularly in the incorporated territories. Areas not incorporated had a population of some 11 million. It comprised of the Polish province of Lublin and parts of the provinces of Warsaw and Krakow. It was initially termed the 'General Government of the Occupied Polish Areas', but in 1940 was renamed the 'General Government'. This large, unincorporated area was the dumping ground for all undesirables. It was here that the first deportations of Poles and Jews were sent in their thousands. By the end of January 1940, the immense problems of simultaneously attempting to relocate Poles, Jews and the ethnic Germans had become such an administrative nightmare that it was agreed that all Jews should be forced to live in ghettos.

A group of Jewish men have been rounded up inside a town by German troops. Many of these hapless people were forced into ghettos.

German troops on the march during the invasion of Russia in June 1941. It would be here that the population would suffer most at the hands of the Nazis.

Another photograph showing German troops on the march during the invasion of Russia in June 1941.

The first of six photographs showing Russian PoWs surrendering to German forces during the invasion of Russia in the summer of 1941. Russian PoWs were used to construct buildings in the death camps, including crematoria and gas chambers.

German Police interrogate a frightened and bewildered old Jewish gentleman. It is more than likely this photograph was taken during a resettlement action.

A photograph depicting a liquidation action of a town.

Jewish people have been loaded into one of the many cattle cars in preparation for them to be sent from the ghettos to one of the Reinhardt concentration camps.

An SS officer confers with his staff during a roll call of political and Jewish prisoners in a camp.

(**Opposite, above**) Wearing their distinctive stripy overalls, Jewish men have been selected for forced labour. (*Auschwitz-Birkenau Museum / Yad Vashem / USHMM*)

(**Above**) Concentration camp forced labour removing earth for the construction of a building.

(**Opposite, below**) Jewish women have been selected for forced labour at Auschwitz-Birkenau and stand at a roll call in front of the camp's kitchen. (*Auschwitz-Birkenau Museum / Yad Vashem / USHMM*)

Chełmno (Kulmhof) – Killing Centre

In the late summer of 1941, SS-Sturmbannführer Herbert Lange, who had already experienced the mass killings of Poles in mobile gas chambers, orchestrated gassing experiments of some 1,500 Jews in gas vans north-east of Chełmno (renamed Kulmhof by Germans). The gassings were a success and the Nazis looked for a suitable place to build an extermination centre in the area. By October a location had been chosen and Lange was made commandant of the new camp. The following month he was given two vans, nicknamed 'Kaisers-Kaffee' vans, manufactured by the Gaubschat factory in Berlin. They had sealed compartments with metal pipes welded below the floor into which the engine exhaust gasses were directed.

The Chełmno site was situated in a run-down castle on an empty manor house estate. All the inhabitants in the area were removed for secrecy. Initially Lange's SS-Sonderkommando that would operate the camp consisted of fifteen members of the security police, fifty policemen of the Kompanie des Polizeibataillons Litzmann-stadt (Łódź), and some policemen who were given Transport, Castle and Forest Camp duties.

Killing operations began on 8 December 1941 when Koło and Romani Jews arrived in lorries. They were stripped of their possessions and herded into the mobile gas vans. The van driver, wearing a gas mask, then connected the exhaust pipe to the chamber. After the occupants had died, the driver made his way to the burial pits in the nearby Rzuchów Forest. The corpses were dragged from the vans and thrown into pits and burned by the 'forest kommando'. The incinerated remains were then covered up.

The camp got through six to nine van-loads per day and over a few weeks 3,830 Koło Jews and 4,000 Romani people were killed this way.

One of the largest communities to be murdered at the Chełmno killing centre were the residents of the Łódź ghetto. Deportations began on 16 January 1942 and proceeded in phases until 15 May 1942. Some 55,000 Jews from the Łódź ghetto were gassed at Chełmno.

Although the killing centre was a success in the eyes of the German authorities, it did not run without incident. One gas van in March 1942 had broken down on a main road with living victims inside. Passers-by heard the cries. It was decided that in future the vans had to be parked while the prisoners were murdered. The following month a van exploded while the driver was revving the engine at the loading bay full of living Jews. The explosion blew off the back doors leaving badly burned and terrified inhabitants inside.

Chełmno continued to operate through the remainder of 1942 and early 1943, killing more people from the Łódź ghetto and surrounding areas of the Warthe-land District. But other death camps, such as Treblinka, Sobibor and Belzec, had more efficient ways of killing and incinerating people.

By March 1943 it was agreed that the Chełmno camp should be closed down. An SS order was sent out outlining that all remains were to be exhumed and burned in open-air crematoria by a unit of Sonderkommando 1005. The bones were then crushed by a special machine and the remains gathered in hundreds of sacks which were emptied into a nearby river. Then the manor house was demolished.

In June 1944, as the last part of the Łódź ghetto was liquidated, a special detachment called 'Bothmann' returned to its old killing grounds and set up a small camp in the Rzuchów Forest consisting of a wooden barracks and new crematory pyres. Over a month the inhabitants of the Łódź ghetto were sent there where Bothmann resumed killing operations using mobile gas vans. Some 25,000 victims were murdered during this action until it was decided to transport the remaining Łódź Jews to Auschwitz-Birkenau. The camp was then closed down for good.

Jews are being unloaded off a train transport by the deportation police (Evakuierungspolizei) destined for the Chełmno extermination camp.

Jewish deportees from the Łódź ghetto, who have been taken to the Chełmno death camp, are transferred from a closed passenger train to a train of open cars at a station.

Elderly women carrying young children and bundles of personal belongings trudge along a street in the Łódź ghetto towards the assembly point for deportations to Chełmno. *(USHMM)*

Jews during a deportation action being sent to a concentration camp.

Photographed during the Międzyrzec Ghetto action are three soldiers and a policeman on the far right. During the two day action around 10,000 Międzyrzec Jews were deported to Treblinka.

(**Opposite, above**) A unit of deportation police poses in the Łódź ghetto in the spring of 1942 preparing to ship Jews to Chełmno. The original German caption reads: 'Evakueringspolizei, spring 1942, #128 [number blurred and hard to read]'. (*USHMM, Robert Abrams*)

(**Opposite, below**) Jewish men and women prepare to sort clothing confiscated from the deportees to the Chełmno death camp. (*USHMM, Sidney Harcsztark*)

(**Above, left**) SS-Hauptscharführer Erwin Burstinge, an SS man on the staff of the Chełmno extermination camp.

(**Above, right**) Two SS concentration camp personnel appearing to enjoy the comradeship in their role. For many of the staff working inside these camps, the prestige of the uniform, elitism, toughness, and comradeship often outweighed any morale scruples they had for their hapless inmates. Some almost enjoyed meting out harsh and often brutal punishments for the slightest infractions of camp rules.

Site at which the SS shot and burned the last forty-five of forty-eight prisoners at Chełmno.

Here children are seen during a deportation action being led away from Łódź ghetto to the death camp at Chełmno.

Appearing to enjoy themselves in the summer of 1942 are a group of Polish workmen and SS at Chełmno.

A post-war photograph showing what a typical mobile gas-van looked like. These vans had sealed compartments with metal pipes welded below the floor into which the engine exhaust was directed. They were tested by the T4 team to ensure there was enough carbon monoxide to kill. However, due to the massive influx of deportees selected to be killed the gas vans could not cope.

Majdanek – Labour & Extermination Camp

Himmler instructed Odilo Globocnik to find a place to build a camp that could hold at least 25,000 Russian PoWs. By October 1941 a location had been found on the outskirts of Lublin called Majdanek. Unlike other camps this site was not in a remote rural location away from the population, but within the city limits. Due to the large numbers of Russian prisoners captured on the Eastern Front it was agreed to extend the camp to hold 50,000 inmates. This figure then rose to 125,000 in November and then again the following month to 150,000, at which point they envisaged expanding the camp to hold 250,000 Russian PoWs.

Work began and by mid-December, with almost half the slave labour force dead, there were barracks for 20,000 people. But after it was big enough to hold 50,000 it was decided to stop because, especially after the Wannsee Conference in January 1942, it was realised that many of those who would enter through the gates at Majdanek would not survive, and it was therefore pointless catering for their needs. In light of this, the camp was refurbished as a killing centre with gas chambers.

Majdanek was also used as a sorting and storage facility for the 'Reinhard death camps': most of the property and valuables taken from the victims of Sobibor, Treblinka and Belzec were sent to Majdanek to be sorted.

At its peak Majdanek boasted seven gas chambers, two wooden gallows, and some 227 structures, placing it among the largest of Nazi concentration camps at that time.

In the spring of 1942, some 8,500 Slovak Jews and 6,000 Jews from the Protectorate of Bohemia and Moravia, including shipments from Germany and Austria, were sent to Majdanek. It was not until the end of August that the first batch of the poisonous gas was delivered to the camp. A month later, gas chamber operations began. There were two identical buildings in the camp where Zyklon-B was used. Carbon monoxide was also used for killing prisoners.

From October 1942 the camp had a contingent of female personnel, known as overseers. They were notoriously cruel, perhaps because they were eager to show their male SS superiors that they could be as brutal as them.

In late 1942, on the orders of Himmler, 35,000 people detained in prisons across the General Government were transported to Majdanek and Auschwitz. The first transport arrived on 7 January 1943 in Lublin. Deportees included political prisoners from Radom, Kielce, Piotrków and Częstochowa. At this time the camp held 10,000 prisoners, of which 7,000 were Jews, and another 1,800 were non-Jewish Poles.

On 27 April 1943 the first transports of Jews from the Warsaw ghetto began arriving, and in June the first transports arrived from Zamosc. The increase in Jewish transports to the camp was in response to 'Aktion Reinhard': the three Reinhard camps were becoming overloaded.

As plans were put into place to kill most of the inhabitants of the camp, body disposal became the greatest issue. The burning of one batch of corpses in one furnace took about one hour. This was insufficient and the camp authorities sought to build more efficient cremation facilities. Earlier in the year Office C of the WVHA notified the Central Construction Board in Lublin that it would send five furnaces as soon as they had been adapted. By July 1943 building work started. It was completed in late August or early September 1943. The crematorium building comprised an office for the head of the crematorium, a hall for corpses, a room with a concrete autopsy table, a coke storage room, and in the main hall of the building five coke-fuelled furnaces. The company which built them – Kori – boasted that incineration would take only 10–15 minutes in these new furnaces.

A few months later, in early November 1943, the camp's newly commissioned crematoria were operating at maximum capacity when it began a killing operation known as 'Harvest Festival'. On one single day, 3 November 1943, 18,400 Jews were murdered. By the end of 'Harvest Festival' Majdanek had only 71 Jews left alive out of 6,562 prisoners.

Between December 1943 and March 1944, Majdanek received some 18,000 so-called 'invalids', many of whom were gassed on arrival using Zyklon B. Executions by firing squad continued as well, with 600 shot on 21 January 1944, 180 shot two days later, and 200 shot on 24 March 1944.

By mid-July the Red Army was fast approaching Lublin, so an evacuation order was sent out giving instructions to destroy the camp and its murder facilities. However, due to the speed of the Russian advance, and the incompetence of the camp's deputy commander, Anton Themes, the camp was evacuated virtually intact. Although some 1,000 inmates were marched to Auschwitz, Soviet forces still found thousands of inmates alive when the camp was liberated.

Jewish men being taken to the Majdanek camp, tied together with ropes around their necks.

(**Above**) Camp entrance gate in 1943 of the Majdanek camp. (*Majdanek-State-Museum / Halfen*)

(**Opposite, above**) A view of the barracks from a watch tower in Majdanek. In mid-October 1942 the camp held 9,519 registered prisoners, of which 7,468 were Jews, and 1,884 were non-Jewish Poles. By August 1943 this figure had become 16,206 prisoners in the main camp, of which 9,105 were Jews and 3,893 were non-Jewish Poles. (*USHMM, Instytut Pamieci Narodowej*)

(**Opposite, below**) An aerial view of the wooden barracks at Majdanek. At the onset of Operation Reinhard the installation was made into a secondary sorting and storage depot for property and valuables taken from the victims at the killing centres of Belzec, Sobibor, and Treblinka. (*USHMM, Panstwowe Muzeum na Majdanku*)

(**Above**) A view of the double fence that surrounded part of the camp. Image taken after liberation in 1944. (*USHMM, Panstwowe Muzeum na Majdanku*)

(**Opposite, above**) A guard post at the entrance to Field III in Majdanek. The camp operated from 1 October 1941 until 22 July 1944 and was virtually intact when the Red Army liberated it. (*USHMM, Instytut Pamieci Narodowej*)

(**Opposite, below**) The first of three photographs showing prisoners at forced labour in the Majdanek concentration camp. The images appear to show prisoners constructing the camp. The initial construction phase commenced with 150 Jewish forced labourers from one of Globocnik's Lublin camps. Later the workforce included 2,000 Russian PoWs. Conditions were so bad that within weeks only 500 were still alive. By mid-December, barracks for 20,000 were ready. (*USHMM, National Archives, Instytut Pamieci Narodowej*)

A view of the crematoria. In July 1943 building work started on the crematoria and was completed in late August or early September 1943. The main crematorium building consisted of an office for the head of the crematorium, a hall for corpses, a room with a concrete autopsy table, a coke storage room, and in the main hall of the building five coke-fuelled furnaces for incinerating bodies. By November 1943, during Operation Harvest Festival, the crematoria were used at maximum capacity. (*USHMM, Panstwowe Muzeum na Majdanku*)

(**Above**) A view of the crematoria and gas chamber in Majdanek through the barbed wire fence.
(*USHMM, unknown Russian archive*)

(**Opposite, above**) A photograph showing the gas chambers. (*USHMM, unknown Russian archive*)

(**Opposite, below**) A can of Zyklon B used in the mass killing of people in the gas chambers of Auschwitz-Birkenau.
(*Auschwitz-Birkenau Museum*)

(**Above**) Majdanek concentration camp, a view from the village Dziesiata. In the background, smoke from burning corpses. Before the crematoria were built, most of the corpses were burnt on huge open pyres that were maintained day and night. (*USHMM, Panstwowe Muzeum na Majdanku*)

(**Opposite, above**) A view of the camp after its liberation. In late July 1944, with Soviet forces approaching the area around Lublin, the German staff at Majdanek speedily evacuated the camp. However, the staff had only succeeded in partly destroying the crematoria, leaving virtually all of the camp including the extensive wooden barracks and watch towers intact when Russian soldiers arrived on 24 July 1944. (*USHMM, unknown Russian archive*)

(**Opposite, below**) Majdanek concentration camp after liberation. The photograph clearly illustrates the size of the camp with its double high fences and wooden sentry towers. (*USHMM, unknown Russian archive*)

(**Above**) A view of the barracks from a watch tower in Majdanek after its liberation. (*USHMM, Instytut Pamieci Narodowej*)

(**Right**) Rapportführer Hermine Braunsteiner, an SS female guard who was a supervising wardress as Majdanek.

(**Opposite**) Six Jewish survivors in front of a crematorium at the Majdanek concentration camp. (*USHMM, Josef Kliger*)

(**Below**) This photograph showing the crematorium ovens at the Majdanek concentration camp after the liberation. Note the bones of the victims. (*USHMM, Leopold Page Photographic Collection, Panstwowe Muzeum na Majdanku*)

Following the liberation of the camp a Russian soldier takes a photograph of the crematorium ovens with piles of bones in front of them. *(USHMM, Panstwowe Muzeum na Majdanku)*

Auschwitz-Birkenau – Labour & Extermination Camp

Oswiecim (Oświęcim) was situated in a remote corner of south-western Poland, in a marshy valley where the Sola River flows into the Vistula about 35 miles west of the ancient city of Krakow. The town was virtually unknown outside Poland and following the occupation of the country Oswiecim was incorporated into the Reich together with Upper Silesia. Here in April 1940 the Nazis built Auschwitz.

Auschwitz was officially a quarantine camp for labour exchange and the nearby town and surrounding area was to be altered beyond recognition. Himmler envisaged that a German settlement at Auschwitz would be built, and from this model town a Germanisation of various villages would be effected.

However, for the time being Auschwitz would remain a concentration camp housing a mixture of inmates consisting of Jews, 'members of the intelligentsia', resistance and political prisoners, and Polish Catholic priests.

On 1 March 1941 Himmler, with high-ranking SS officers, political leaders of Silesia, and the officers of the giant chemical conglomerate IG Farben met to hear that a site had been chosen for an extension to Auschwitz near the village of Brzezinka, a marshy tract of land surrounded by birch woods about 2 miles west of the main camp. The houses of the village were cleared in July and its inhabitants relocated. The Germans named the area Birkenau.

The task of designing Birkenau was left in the hands of SS-Hauptsturmführer Karl Bischoff, the newly appointed chief of the Auschwitz construction office, and the 33-year-old architect SS-Rottenführer Fritz Ertl. The budget for the construction was to be 8.9 million Reich Marks. The projected number of prisoners to be housed in the camp was 97,000. It was planned that Birkenau would be divided into a two-part camp, with the smaller part of only 17,000 inmates located in a quarantine camp. The inmates were to be packed in, with one barrack block designed to contain 550 inmates. In the end they managed to accommodate 744.

Within weeks Birkenau began taking shape. Some 140,000 cubic feet of earth was excavated, 1,600 concrete foundations laid, 600 concrete posts erected for the fence with 100,000 feet of barbed wire, and 86,000 cubic feet of brickwork using more than a million bricks. The barracks, standard army horse-stable barracks made by a German company, would be produced and dispatched to Auschwitz in kit form. They could be assembled very rapidly by a gang of thirty unskilled men led by one carpenter. In total 253 of these huts were assigned to Birkenau. By the end of 1941 the area had been transformed from a quiet backwater into one of the largest concentration camp systems of the Reich.

To start with Auschwitz was a camp in which Russian PoWs lived and worked. However, soon the Russian PoWs were replaced by Jews, the first transports arriving in February 1942. Those deemed unfit for labour were sent to the new modified gas chamber and murdered.

There were so many to murder that planners decided to build a new facility at Birkenau. It was proposed that a cottage at the far end of the camp be converted. It was known as Bunker I and nicknamed 'the little red house'. Its windows and doors were bricked up, cracks were sealed to make it air tight, and the interior gutted to form two rooms. The doors to both rooms had signs over the entrance: 'Zur Desinfektion' (to disinfection). Bunker I was to function along similar lines to that of the main camp but on a grander scale. It was completed in a few weeks and on 20 March 1942 it gassed it first Jews – a shipment from Upper Silesia.

Soon plans were made to convert a second cottage, the 'little white house', into a 'bathing facility for special actions'. Bunker II went into operation at the end of June. It consisted of four narrow rooms constructed as gas chambers. With better ventilation and a killing capacity of around 1,200 people a time, Höss, the commandant, was sure that Birkenau would run more efficiently than ever.

However, there was the problem of body disposal. With no proper crematoria yet built, thousands of bodies from both cottages would be collected from the gas chamber entrance, loaded onto trucks and driven to a nearby pit and dumped. But this was soon found to be impractical: there were too many bodies and they could not be buried deep enough. So an improvised crematorium was built and prisoners were forced to dig up the bodies and burn them in the temporary crematorium.

Now construction of crematoria began in earnest. The SS brought in eleven construction companies to build them and several hundred workers were allocated to assist. The civilian firm of Huta from Katowice worked on the shell of Crematorium II and then began work on Crematorium IV. The local Auschwitz contractor Koehler worked on the chimneys while Topf and Sons built the furnaces of Crematoriums IV and V. Huta completed the floor and walls of the two underground morgues of Crematorium II, while the Vedag Company from Breslau were paid to waterproof the cellars of Crematorium II and III.

Showing the infamous gates of 'Arbeit Macht Frei' ('work sets you free'). The commandant of Auschwitz, Rudolf Hoss, firmly believed that inmates gained a sense of discipline by working during their imprisonment, and this discipline would enable them to withstand the harsh environment of prison life. He believed that endless labour brought about a kind of spiritual freedom. (*HITM courtesy of Auschwitz-Birkenau State Museum*)

Taken from within Auschwitz I camp looking out towards the main gate and security office. In 1940, this entrance was where political prisoners would be led through to start their imprisonment. (*HITM courtesy of Auschwitz-Birkenau State Museum*)

In March 1943 Crematoria II and IV went into operation and by this time with the growing amount of shipments pouring through to Birkenau there was great urgency to complete the other two crematoria. By the summer of 1943 all of the crematoria were running in spite of some technical issues.

The transports into Birkenau became ever larger, more transports arriving daily through 1943. In the spring of 1944 the numbers arriving at Auschwitz would reach its peak with a huge assignment of Hungarians Jews.

(**Above**) Showing the high tension electric fence in Auschwitz I with a sign that reads 'Caution, High Voltage, Danger to Life'. On the left are prisoner blocks and on the right is the commandant's office, camp administration office and the SS hospital. In 1940, most of the buildings in the camp were intended to house and provide the basic needs for the prisoners, guards and SS staff that ran the camp. (*HITM courtesy of Auschwitz-Birkenau State Museum*)

(**Opposite, above**) At Auschwitz I, showing what one of the three crematoria furnaces looked like during its operation at the camp. The crematoria, known as Crematoria I, operated from 15 August 1940 until July 1943. According to German reports, some 340 corpses could be burned every 24-hours after the installation of the three furnaces. (*HITM courtesy of Auschwitz-Birkenau State Museum*)

(**Opposite, below**) In its present state showing the north-west side of Crematorium I in Auschwitz I. In September 1944, the crematorium was shut down, its chimney removed and was converted into an air raid shelter for the SS hospital. The chimney was rebuilt in 1946/47. Note the steel-faced, gas-tight door with peephole.
(*HITM courtesy of Auschwitz-Birkenau State Museum*)

Taken inside one of the SS offices at the Auschwitz main camp. (*Auschwitz-Birkenau Museum*)

Prisoners digging trenches for heating or plumbing pipes near the main reception building (Aufnahmegebäude) in Auschwitz I. (*Auschwitz-Birkenau Museum*)

Construction works by the main entrance to Birkenau, the photo taken from the internal part of the camp, possibly spring/summer 1943. In May 1944 Höss would supervise the laying of a railway line through the main entrance for Action Höss, the operation for transporting primarily Hungarian Jews to Birkenau. (*Auschwitz-Birkenau Museum*)

Two photographs showing prisoners digging drainage ditches in Birkenau. (*Auschwitz-Birkenau Museum*)

Prefabricated wooden stable barracks at B II of the Birkenau camp, winter 1943/4. (*Auschwitz-Birkenau Museum*)

(**Opposite, above**) The construction of Crematorium IV taken by SS-man Kamann in late 1942. The architects signed off Crematorium IV on 22 March 1943 without having time to test the incinerators. After two weeks of intensive use the double four muffle furnace cracked. The incinerator was decommissioned in May 1943. (*Auschwitz-Birkenau Museum*)

(**Above**) Höss (front row raised left arm) accompanies Himmler with engineer Faust and other officials to inspect the construction site of IG-Farben in Monowitz on 18 July 1942. (*Auschwitz-Birkenau Museum*)

(**Opposite, below**) Taken in August 1942 showing SS-Sturmbannführer Karl Bischoff and SS-Untersturmführer Walter Dejaco, head of the drawing office, conferring with the aid of a blueprint in the initial stages of construction at the Crematoria IV and V sites. In the background civilian workers, probably from the firm Lenz & Co, which specialised in site-levelling work. (*Auschwitz-Birkenau Museum*)

(**Opposite, above**) SS sentries during a ceremony. In 1940 there were some 250 SS guards at Auschwitz-Birkenau; by March 1941 that figure had risen to 700; within three months it was around 2,000; in April 1944 the number was 2,950; in August, 3340; and by January 1945 it had reached 4,480. (*Auschwitz-Birkenau Museum*)

(**Above**) Between spring 1942 and mid-1944 this was the area where trains with deported Jews halted. (*Auschwitz-Birkenau Museum*)

(**Opposite, below**) The ramps of Birkenau have been cleared of Hungarian Jews and their belongings have been collected together. In the distance the twin chimneys of Crematoria II and III can be seen to the left and right of the two trains. (*Auschwitz-Birkenau Museum*)

(**Above**) A transport from Subcarpathian Rus is taken off the trains and assembled on the ramp at Auschwitz-Birkenau. Many of these Jews were deported from Berehovo, where Jews from neighbouring towns and villages were gathered at a brick factory. This photograph is from the album, which includes 193 photographs mounted on 56 pages, of SS-Hauptscharführer Bernhardt Walter, head of the Auschwitz photographic laboratory known as the Erkennungsdienst (Identification Service) and his assistant SS-Unterscharführer Ernst Hofmann. The album was produced as a presentation volume for the camp commandant. (*Auschwitz-Birkenau Museum*)

(**Opposite, above**) Jews from Subcarpathian Rus undergo a selection on the ramp at Auschwitz-Birkenau. Pictured in front holding a riding crop may be either SS Unterscharführer Wilhelm Emmerich or SS Hauptsturmführer Georg Höcker assisted by the Jewish prisoner Hans Schorr. (*Auschwitz-Birkenau Museum*)

(**Opposite, below**) Jews from Subcarpathian Rus undergo a selection on the ramp at Auschwitz-Birkenau in May 1944. (*Auschwitz-Birkenau Museum*)

(**Opposite, above**) Newly arrived Jews from Subcarpathian Rus get off the train in Auschwitz-Birkenau. (*Auschwitz-Birkenau Museum*)

(**Opposite, below**) Jews from Subcarpathian Rus sit in a large group on the ramp at Auschwitz-Birkenau before undergoing the selection process. One of the crematoria is visible in the distance on the right. (*Auschwitz-Birkenau Museum*)

(**Above**) A transport of Jews from Subcarpathian Rus is taken off the trains and assembled on the ramp at Auschwitz-Birkenau. (*Auschwitz-Birkenau Museum*)

(**Opposite, above**) SS guards supervise the arrival of a transport of Jews from Subcarpathian Rus to Auschwitz-Birkenau. Pictured on the far right is SS Wachmann Stefan Baretzki. Baretzki was conscripted into the SS and stationed at the Auschwitz concentration camp from 1942 until 1945. There he participated in mass murder by making selections, and was unrestrained in his beating of prisoners. (*Auschwitz-Birkenau Museum*)

(**Above**) Babo Batren, an elderly Jewish woman from Tecso, leans against the deportation train in Auschwitz-Birkenau while waiting to be taken to the gas chambers. (*Auschwitz-Birkenau Museum*)

(**Opposite, below**) Jewish women and children from Subcarpathian Rus who have been selected for death at Auschwitz-Birkenau wait to be taken to the gas chambers. (*Auschwitz-Birkenau Museum*)

(**Opposite, above**) Jews from Subcarpathian Rus await selection on the ramp at Auschwitz-Birkenau. (*Auschwitz-Birkenau Museum*)

(**Above**) A group of religious Jews from Subcarpathian Rus wait on the ramp at Auschwitz-Birkenau. (*Auschwitz-Birkenau Museum*)

(**Opposite, below**) Jews from Subcarpathian Rus undergo a selection on the ramp at Auschwitz-Birkenau. The selection was often carried out by one or two SS medical doctors. The deportees were divided into four columns: two of women and children, and two of men. Those unfit for labour were sent straight to the crematoria, while the able-bodied workers were interned in Auschwitz, or were retained ready at a moment's notice to be transferred to other camps in the Reich. The selection for labour in each transport varied daily; sometimes it was 10 per cent, sometimes it was 50 per cent. But most of the Jews that arrived through the gates of Birkenau were immediately sent to the 'bathhouses' to their deaths. (*Auschwitz-Birkenau Museum*)

Jewish women and children who have been selected for death walk in a line towards the gas chambers. The gate at the upper left leads to the section of the camp on the south side of the ramp known as BI. *(Auschwitz-Birkenau Museum)*

Jewish women and children from Subcarpathian Rus who have been selected for death at Auschwitz-Birkenau wait to be taken to the gas chambers. *(Auschwitz-Birkenau Museum)*

Two photographs showing Jewish women and children from Subcarpathian Rus who have been selected for death at Auschwitz-Birkenau walking to the gas chambers. *(Auschwitz-Birkenau Museum)*

(**Above**) A transport of Jews from Subcarpathian Rus is taken off the trains and assembled on the ramp at Auschwitz-Birkenau. (*Auschwitz-Birkenau Museum*)

(**Opposite, above**) Jews from Subcarpathian Rus undergo a selection on the ramp at Auschwitz-Birkenau. SS officers regularly watched the shipments arrive and became morbidly fascinated by the spectacle. They witnessed the selection process at the unloading ramps and saw for themselves the awful scenes of families being torn apart and the separating of the men from the women and children. (*Auschwitz-Birkenau Museum*)

(**Opposite, below**) Jewish men from Subcarpathian Rus await selection on the ramp at Auschwitz-Birkenau. (*Auschwitz-Birkenau Museum*)

(**Above**) Jewish women and children from Subcarpathian Rus await selection on the ramp at Auschwitz-Birkenau. (*Auschwitz-Birkenau Museum*)

(**Opposite, above**) Jewish men from Subcarpathian Rus await selection on the ramp at Auschwitz-Birkenau. (*Auschwitz-Birkenau Museum*)

(**Opposite, below**) Jewish women and children from Subcarpathian Rus who have been selected for death at Auschwitz-Birkenau walk towards the gas chambers. The building in the background is Crematorium III. In May 1944 on average 3,300 Hungarian Jews arrived per day. On 20 May, for instance, one convoy arrived with 3,000 people, of whom some 1,000 were able and 2,000 were unable to work. The next day two convoys were reported to have arrived from Hungary with 6,000 people, of whom 2,000 were able to work and the remainder were sent directly to their deaths. That day both the incinerators of Crematoria II and III were being serviced so the victims from the transport were disposed of in the three incineration ditches next to Crematorium V. Though the specially built track from the crematorium to the pits had been laid it was never used because it was considered an inconvenience. (*Auschwitz-Birkenau Museum*)

Two photographs showing disinfected and shorn female prisoners after leaving the Central Sauna. After being shorn, disinfected and showered under the surveillance of the SS, they were then given their disinfected and disinfested clothes and escorted to their designated barracks with a blanket for their bunk. Being shaved and stripped the new prisoners lost the last vestiges of their identity. They now all looked alike. (*Auschwitz-Birkenau Museum*)

Chapter Two

The Reinhard Camps

At the Wannsee conference held in Berlin in January 1942 it was agreed that it would be the Jews in the General Government that would be dealt with first. Preparations had already been made and the Nazi leadership was under no illusion that it required great organizational skills to deal with the necessary mass murder effectively. A pool of experts had been drafted in to undertake this mammoth task. They knew that transporting large numbers of Jews to Russia and killing them would be a logistical nightmare, especially when the war in Russia had not been won. They soon came to the conclusion that it was more practical to transport German and other Jews to Poland and kill them immediately rather than send them further East. It was therefore suggested that a series of camps be constructed in Poland, used primarily to transport those deemed unfit for work and kill them.

Operation Reinhard was the codename for the systematic annihilation of the Polish Jews in the General Government, and it would mark the beginning of the use of extermination camps. The SS and police leader of Lublin, SS-Oberstgruppenführer Odilo Globocnik, was appointed the commander of the operation. He was a ruthless and fanatical SS officer who believed wholeheartedly in the Nazi vision. In his office he gossiped with his associates about the future SS colonization of the East and planned the task of exterminating the Jews in the General Government.

Globocnik brought in people who had been assigned to the euthanasia program who had the knowledge and experience of setting up and operating factories for mass murder. Three death camps were proposed: Belzec, Sobibor, and Treblinka.

Belzec

The first of the Reinhard camps was located in the south-east of the district of Lublin and called Belzec/Bełżec. It was situated 500 metres from the station siding. It was divided into two parts: Camp I on the north-west side containing the reception area with two barracks – one for undressing and where the women had their hair shorn and the other for storing clothes and luggage. Camp II comprised the gas chambers, a large area for mass graves, and two barracks for the Jewish work details, one as living quarters and one containing a kitchen. The gas chambers were surrounded by trees and had camouflage nets on the roofs. Camps I and II were dived by a wire fence. The barracks for undressing and the gas chambers were linked by an enclosed path 2 metres wide known as the 'tube' which was concealed on each side by a wire fence and foliage. The whole camp was topped with barbed wire and camouflaged with newly planted conifers. The camp was overlooked by two wooden watch towers.

The camp was to be guarded by eighty guards, all Ukrainian. Famed for their brutality, many of these Ukrainians had previously fought the Red Army and were now to be trained by the Germans for an opportunity to escape the terrible PoW camps. They were all trained at Trawniki, a camp near Lublin set up for the purpose. These volunteers were nicknamed by the local population 'Trawniki men' or 'Askaries'. The Germans called them 'Hilfswillige' (willing helpers) or 'hiwis' for short.

The camp commandant, Christian Wirth, had arrived at Belzec before Christmas 1941, bringing with him a group of about ten 'euthanasia' specialists, including the notorious chemist Dr Kallmeyer. They had been given the task of constructing the gassing facility and then operating it. Wirth had been involved in the T4 euthanasia in 1939. Two years later he was dispatched to Lublin where he continued his killings. Wirth soon earned himself a reputation and was nicknamed the 'savage Christian'.

In February 1942 two gassing tests were undertaken at Belzec, the first with Zyklon B [cyanide gas] and the second with bottled carbon monoxide. As a cheaper alternative a Soviet tank engine was installed to produce carbon monoxide from exhaust gas which was fed into the chamber. The technique was a complete success and there was now no need to export CO gas to this distant part of Poland.

Wirth realized that by killing large numbers of people in one place he had broken from the conventional design of a concentration camp. Because the vast majority of arrivals would be alive only for a matter of hours, a complex of buildings such as those at Auschwitz would no longer be required. A death camp, unlike a concentration camp, needed only a few facilities to operate effectively.

Wirth had the gas chamber building hidden behind trees to conceal the true purpose of the place from the new arrivals for as long as possible.

He would select a number of healthy Jewish slave labourers who would be put to work burying bodies, sorting clothing and valuables, and cleaning the gas chambers.

The Belzec death camp began operations on 17 March 1942 with a transport of fifty goods wagons containing Jews from Lublin. Between March and the end of April, thousands of Jews from the Lublin and Lemberg districts were exterminated in Belzec. Himmler sent his congratulations to Wirth who had finally built a killing factory capable of murdering many hundreds of thousands of people in one place. Wirth looked upon the operation as a factory to which raw goods were delivered, processed and then stored. Wirth was helping to realize his Führer's dream of the annihilation of the Jewish race.

In March another 'Reinhard' death camp was being constructed near the village of Sobibor.

A photograph showing Belzec station entrance.

Escorted Jews on the way to Belzec death camp.

Following a deportation action to Belzec a number of men can be seen examining luggage left behind by the transport. The Jews were told that their possessions would follow on after their departure, but this was to dupe them into believing they would be resettled. As we know, they were sent with the sole intention of being murdered.

Jews at Belzec constructing tank trap fortifications.

An SS man at the Belzec camp, posing in front of the flour mill, which was used as an assembly place for Jews deported to the camp.

(**Above**) Close-up of a Romani couple sitting in an open area in the Belzec concentration camp. (*USHMM, Jerzy Ficowski*)

(**Opposite, above**) SS man Rudolf or 'Rudi' Kamm outside the barracks at Belzecrudi Kamm – Belzec. Most of the SS camp personnel first worked in the euthanasia programme (Aktion T4).

(**Opposite, below**) SS man Erwin Fichtner has emerged from the main administration office in Belzec. On the right is the armoury building. At Belzec he was the camp quartermaster. He was killed by Polish partisans on 29 March 1943, not far from the camp.

(**Above**) A portrait photo of SS Ernst Schemmel. Initially he was employed at the T4 Institute at Pirna, Sonnenstein and Hartheim. He was then given a post to Belzec, and then served at Treblinka from late September to early October 1942, where he acted as a deputy for commandant Franz Stangl.

(**Opposite, above**) View of the home of the commandant of the Belzec concentration camp, located a short distance from the camp. (*USHMM, Instytut Pamieci Narodowej*)

(**Opposite, below**) Nearest the camera from left to right: (1) SS-Rottenführer Fritz Tauscher (committed suicide in prison in 1965), (2) SS-Rottenführer Karl Gringer (fate unknown), (3) SS-Rottenführer Ernst Zierke (arrested for war crimes in 1963, acquitted in 1965), (4) SS-Hauptscharführer Lorenz Hackenholt (disappeared after the war), (5) Polizei Wachtmeister Arthur Dachsel (his fate unknown), (6) SS-Rottenführer Heinrich Barbl (thought to have survived the war).

Group portrait of Trawniki-trained guards at Belzec killing centre, 1942. Trawniki men, Trawnikimänner, were central and east European collaborators recruited from Russian PoW camps. Apart from assisting the Germans in military operations, the Trawnikis took a major part in the extermination process of the Jews, including rounding them up from the ghettos and deporting them to the concentration camps. *(USHMM, Instytut Pamieci Narodowej)*

Sobibor

The Sobibor death camp was constructed in a wooded area on the Chełmno–Włodawa railway line. The installation was an enlarged and improved version of Belzec with the same general layout. SS-Hauptsturmführer Franz Stangl, aged 34, was appointed commandant. He was the son of a night-watchman and in the 1930s was accepted into the Austrian police service. Later he claimed he liked the cleanliness of the police uniforms and security they offered. After the annexation of Austria, Stangl rose quickly through the ranks. In 1940, through an order of Himmler, he became superintendent of the T4 Euthanasia Programme at Schloss Hartheim. Here Stangl met Wirth. In 1971 he said of him: 'He addressed us daily at lunch … he spoke about the necessity for this euthanasia operation … he spoke of "doing away with useless mouths" and … that "sentimental slobber made him puke".' By the time Stangl received his new appointment Wirth had become commander of both Chełmno and Belzec, and was soon to oversee Stangl's operation at Sobibor.

Before Stangl's appointment to Sobibor he had to report to SS HQ in Lublin where he met Gruppenführer Odilo Globocnik who was directing the extermination of Jews in Poland. For almost three hours on a park bench Globocnik went through the plans of the new camp, but never told Stangl that the new installation was an extermination centre for Jews. When Stangl arrived at Sobibor it still resembled a building site. He was informed that Wirth had been appointed inspector of the camps and that he had to report to him immediately. He journeyed by car to Belzec, which was now in full operation. 'As one arrived, one first reached Belzec railway station, on the left side of the road', Stangl recalled. 'The camp was on the same side, but up a hill. The Kommandantur was 200 metres away, on the other side of the road. It was a one storey building. The smell …' he said, 'Oh my God, the smell. It was everywhere. Wirth wasn't in his office. I remember they took me to him … he was standing on a hill, next to the pits … the pits … full … they were full. I can't tell you; not hundreds, thousands, thousands of corpses … oh God. That's where Wirth told me – he said that was what Sobibor was for. And he was putting me officially in charge.'

When Wirth visited Belzec the camp was in turmoil. One of the pits was over-flowing with corpses and the gassing installation was perpetually breaking down. The deportees were waiting to be gassed naked and without food or water sometimes for days. Others were left in the railway wagons, many suffocating as a result.

Wirth told Stangl that the problems at Belzec were caused by a massive influx of deportees and that the gas vans could not cope. Stangl claimed he was shocked at the terrible conditions and the suffering of those awaiting their fate outside the gas chambers, but that he was embraced by the structure of allegiance and returned to Sobibor to undertake his duty as commandant of an extermination centre.

When the gas chamber had been completed Stangl was ordered to witness his first gassing: 'When I got there Wirth stood in front of the building wiping the sweat off his cap and fuming. Michel told me later that he'd suddenly appeared, looked around the gas chambers on which they were still working and said, "Right, we'll try it out now with those twenty-five work Jews: get them up here." They marched our twenty-five Jews up there and just pushed them in and gassed them. Michel said Wirth behaved like a lunatic, hit out at his own staff with his whip to drive them on. And then he was livid because the doors hadn't worked properly.'

Sobibor officially became operational in mid-May 1942. Within the first two months some 100,000 people were killed there. Often Stangl appeared at the unloading ramps dressed in white riding clothes watching as the Ukrainian guards flung open the doors and chased the people out of the wagons with their leather whips. Instructions came from a loudspeaker: 'undress completely, including artificial limbs and spectacles. Give your valuables up at the counter. Tie your shoes together carefully.' Then women and girls were herded into a building to be shorn, and their shaved hair put into potato sacks. Then the deportees were moved along a path to their death. After they had been murdered, from the gas chamber entrance the corpses would be loaded onto a truck and driven to the pit and dumped. Powdered lime would be thrown over the bodies before they were covered with soil.

Summer 1942 was particularly hot and dry and as a result the buried corpses started to putrefy. The rotting bodies began rising to the surface and there was a terrible stench across the camp. Plagues of rats too were seen gnawing at the corpses. The whole area was covered with swarms of flies and where the decomposed bodies had been dumped traces of stinking body fluids oozed out of the holes.

By the summer of 1942, both Sobibor and Belzec were in operation, and despite the problems, the 'Reinhard' camps were achieving what they had been intended for, the mass extermination of the Jews.

While Sobibor and Belzec continued to operate at full capacity, a far bigger installation was being prepared to receive all transports from the Warsaw and Bialystok ghettos. The site chosen was near the village of Treblinka in the north-eastern part of the General Government.

Jews during a deportation action during the Reinhardt operation. By the summer of 1942 thousands of Jews were being transported across Poland to one of the Reinhardt camps to their death.

Jewish men, women and children are being unloaded from a cattle car during a deportation action to one of the Reinhardt camps in the summer of 1942.

Jews are being transported to Treblinka from Przyrów Ghetto in September 1942.

Photo taken most probably in 1942 showing SS officers overseeing the operation at the camp. The ramp is still visible from the station, the fence not yet built. It is not clear who is leaving the cattle cars in the background.

The following photographs are from a recently-unearthed collection given to the USHMM in January 2020. They are black-and-white, some in two albums and some loose. There are also dozens of documents that chronicle Johann Niemann's background, his family, and his SS career, culminating in his role as deputy commander of the Sobibor death camp. The collection traces Niemann's advancement through the concentration camp system (Esterwegen and Sachsenhausen) and the T4 euthanasia program (Grafeneck, Brandenburg, and Bernburg) to the Operation Reinhard death camps (Belzec and Sobibor). The collection includes the first photographs to come to light showing SS leaders and their auxiliaries at the Sobibor killing centre, some of which are shown here. Niemann was killed by prisoners in the October 1943 Sobibor uprising.

The fence at the entrance of Sobibor was covered with tree branches to camouflage the mass-murder operation. *(USHMM)*

The man in the middle of the photo appears to be a member of the railway staff, flanked by two Trawniki guards posing for the camera in front of the Sobibor station. It was here that the guards and SS personnel unloaded wagons with their victims for extermination. The station building housed a ticket office, a waiting room and a buffet with alcohol licence serving travellers. Strangely, it was used by local residents and members of the camp staff.

Thoroughly enjoying themselves are a group of SS men who served at Sobibor and Treblinka

Niemann, as deputy commandant of Sobibor, often greeted new prisoners. Here he poses on horseback at the arrival ramp. (*USHMM*)

Allegedly, this photographs depicts workers at Sobibor building another structure in the camp.

A group of Sobibor SS personnel can be seen conversing.

Niemann (left) stands with SS-Unterscharführer Adolf Müller in front of a well in the Erbhof (the family farm) in Sobibor in the summer of 1943. (*USHMM*)

(**Opposite, above**) Taking a break from murdering are (from left to right) Arthur Dachsel, possibly Erich Schulze, Niemann, Franz Reichleitner, an unidentified member of the border guard, and Erich Bauer, on the terrace on the new officers' dining room, the Kasino. (*USHMM*)

(**Opposite, below**) View of the Vorlager (living quarters) from the watchtower at the Sobibor camp entrance in the spring of 1943. Identifiable in the background are the roofs of Camp I and the arm of the excavator, which starting work in the autumn of 1942 removing bodies for cremation from the former mass graves in Camp III. (*USHMM*)

(**Above**) From left to right: SS-Unterscharführer Rudolf Kamm, Willi Wendland, Heinrich Unverhau with an accordion, possibly Fritz Konrad, and Johann Klier stand in the Vorlager at Sobibor, early summer 1943. On the right the new officers dining room is visible. Unverhau had recently moved from Belzec to Sobibor, was a trained musician, and supervised Jewish prisoners in the sorting barracks and forest commando. (*USHMM*)

Unverhau with violin, Kamm, possibly Fritz Konrad, Willi Wendland, and Johann Klier on the terrace of the new officers' dining room in Sobibor in the early summer of 1943. (*USHMM*)

Wendland (left) and Wolf playing chess in front of the new officers' dining room at Sobibor in 1943. Franz Wolf came to the camp in the spring of that year. (*USHMM*)

Arthur Dachsel, possibly Erich Schulze, Niemann, Reichleitner, and Erich Bauer (from left to right) enjoying the summer day on the terrace of the new officers' dining room. (*USHMM*)

Franz Reichleitner stands smiling next to an unidentified woman on the dining room terrace. Next to Erich Bauer is Niemann. Reichleitner had been camp commandant since September 1942. (*USHMM*)

This photograph was taken at the Vorlager. It shows Niemann and an unidentified SS-Unterscharführer with two German shepherd dogs. When the deportation trains arrived, the dogs spread terror among the Jews. In the background to the left are the barracks for the Trawniki, and the gable of the former forester's house. The wooden fence surrounds the undressing place for the deportees in Sobibor Camp II. The former forester's house was situated in the grounds of the Erbhof and served as living quarters for a few SS as well as administrative buildings. (USHMM)

SS-Unterscharführer Rudolf Kamm with a German shepherd dog in the summer of 1943. Kamm was originally recruited from the Sonnenstein euthanasia centre where he burned corpses. In the autumn of 1942 he came to Sobibor from Belzec where he was put in charge of the sorting barracks. (USHMM)

A view of the Vorlager. The building on the left served as the officers' dining room and accommodation for Johann Niemann. Between the dining room building and the laundry to the right there was an entrance to the cellar storeroom. These buildings were constructed by forced labourers from the camp. (USHMM)

The funeral of the SS personnel killed in the Sobibor Uprising, where twelve SS personnel were killed. Following the revolt, which took place on 14 October 1943, the camp ceased operations.

SS-Hauptsturmführer Franz Stangl, commandant of Sobibor, enjoying himself with staff. (*H.E.A.R.T.*)

Treblinka

The Treblinka death camp was situated amongst a maze of railway lines in a dense pine forest. Planners had selected the area because the woods concealed the camp from the Malkinia–Kosov road to its north and the Malkinia–Siedlce railway to its west. Just to the south-west a railway line connected Treblinka station with a gravel quarry. The quarry had already been used by the SS for raw materials and a slave labour force had been put to work there. In the summer of 1941 the SS established a labour camp called Treblinka I where a thousand Polish and Jewish detainees lived and worked. The 'labour camp Treblinka' was established by the ordinance of the Governor of the Warsaw district on 15 November 1941. The gravel mine was run by a Deutschen Erd und Steinwerk GmbH.

In April 1942 an SS team arrived at Treblinka. The area did not inspire the small committee of officers, half of which had never been to Poland. They were not impressed by the town with its dreary buildings and hut-like dwellings, but they concentrated on the job in hand: that of finding a suitable location for a death camp.

The plan of the camp was almost identical to Sobibor, but with some improvements. On 1 June 1942 the Central Construction Office of the Waffen-SS and Police in Warsaw dispatched a document confirming plans to commence construction of the new camp immediately.

The contractors assigned were Schönbronn of Leipzig and Schmidt-Münstermann of Warsaw. In charge of construction was SS-Obersturmführer Richard Thomalla, who had completed the building contract at Sobibor and been replaced there by Stangl in April 1942. It took eight weeks. The workers were mostly Jews, transported from neighbouring villages. There were also a number of Poles from nearby Treblinka I. SS-Untersturmführer Heinz Auerswald from the office of the commissioner of the Warsaw ghetto supplied most of the construction materials. As well as using local businesses, he obtained wood from the surrounding forests and sand and gravel from the nearby pit. The site was approximately 13 hectares.

Thomalla ordered that two sets of fences and barbed-wire obstacles be erected first. The main footings and the construction of the brick and wood buildings would then be built. The inner fence was 4 metres high. A contractor was brought in to cover the fence with foliage and tree branches to hide the camp from outside view. A second fence was built 45 metres from the first; it included chains of anti-tank obstacles wrapped in barbed wire. Between the fences an area of land was left barren, devoid of any vegetation. This was done to give the guards maximum visual surveillance of the area so that prisoners could not hide. Fences also surrounded the area within the camp, and at each corner of the installation 8-metre high watch towers were constructed.

The camp was divided into three areas: administration and staff living; reception area; and extermination area. The first two were known as the 'lower camp' while the extermination area was known as the 'upper camp'. Planners had ensured that the Upper Camp was completely separate from the other areas and was camouflaged to prevent observation from outside. The upper camp measured 200 × 250 metres.

The gas chambers were inside a huge brick building that had been built at considerable speed. There were three gas chambers measuring 5 × 5 metres by 2.6 metres in height. The construction was similar to that of the gas chambers constructed at Sobibor. Attached to the main brick building was a smaller building that contained a petrol-driven engine which introduced the CO gas through pipes into the chambers. Installed next to the engine was a diesel generator that supplied electricity to the camp.

The camp was ready for operation in July. The camp personnel, wearing the grey uniforms of the Waffen-SS but without the symbols of their native units, began arriving to take up their new posts at the place known to them as 'TII'. The main personnel had been recruited from the T4 euthanasia centre.

On 22 July Treblinka railway station received a telegram saying that trains would start to run between Warsaw and Treblinka. It said that the trains would have sixty closed cars each and that they would be transporting deportees from the Warsaw ghetto.

The first transport of Jews from the Warsaw ghetto left Malkinia for Treblinka in the early morning of 23 July. By the end of August an estimated 300,000 people had been murdered at Treblinka. The commandant, Dr Irmfried Eberl, was inordinately proud – on some days over 10,000 had been killed.

However, in spite of the huge killing rate, the camp was being run chaotically. There were so many shipments to the camp that Eberl and his staff could not cope. Hundreds of bodies were lying all around and piles of clothes were strewn every-where. SS soldiers and Ukrainian guards standing on the roofs of barracks fired indiscriminately into the crowds, which caused panic and further disorder, especially with new arrivals.

Eberl was dismissed from his post to be replaced by Stangl from Sobibor. Stangl reorganized the camp and got the killing operation running smoothly. New gas chambers were constructed comprising six gas chambers each 4 × 8 metres. The designers ensured that these new structures would be more efficient. The height of the new gas chamber rooms was slightly lower to reduce the amount of gas required and shorten asphyxiation time. In the old chambers there had been instances where young children had not been suffocated properly because the gas had risen to the ceiling.

Those entering the building found it decorated with plants, and the entrance to the corridor was covered by a thick Jewish ceremonial curtain pillaged from a synagogue. On it was inscribed in Hebrew: 'This is the Gateway to God. Righteous men will pass through.' Over the entrance to the door was a large Star of David. To access the door, one climbed five wide steps with potted plants on either side. There was a double-glazed peephole in the door.

The new gas chambers were capable of murdering 2,300 people in six gas chambers simultaneously; the old ones could only murder 680.

The first transport to Treblinka under Stangl's command arrived from Warsaw on 4 September 1942. Between October and the end of December Treblinka reached its peak operation: on some days 20,000 people were murdered. Initially they were mostly Jews from Warsaw, but later many arrived from Germany and other parts of Western Europe.

At Christmas Stangl ordered the construction of a fake railway station at Treblinka. Originally the train platform where the deportees arrived was literally a ramp. But now he wanted to fool the new arrivals into believing they had arrived at a genuine station to a transit camp. This was especially for those arriving from outside Poland, mainly from the west. A clock was painted with numerals and hands that never moved, a ticket-window was constructed, and various timetables and arrows indicating train connections were painted on the walls.

Jews are led through the streets of Warsaw to the railway station following the collapse of the Warsaw Ghetto uprising. Many of these inhabitants of the ghetto were transported directly to Treblinka. (*NARA*)

(**Above**) A photograph taken showing SS troops arresting the Jewish department heads of the Brauer armament factory. The original German caption reads: 'The Jewish department heads of the armament firm Brauer'. *(NARA)*

(**Opposite, above**) A group of Jewish people have been arrested and some interrogated following the Warsaw Ghetto uprising. *(NARA)*

(**Opposite, below**) Jews captured during the suppression of the Warsaw ghetto uprising are led away from the burning ghetto by SS guards. The original German caption reads: 'Pulled from the bunkers by force.' *(NARA)*

(**Above, left**) A photograph of the second commandant of Treblinka, SS-Hauptsturmführer Franz Stangl. Stangl was a 34-year-old Austrian graduate of Hartheim's 'euthanasia' centre. He became commandant of Sobibor death camp before replacing the first commandant, SS-Obersturmführer Dr Irmfried Eberl at Treblinka in the summer of 1942.

(**Above, centre**) SS-Oberscharführer Kurt Franz, Stangl's deputy at Treblinka. Before the war Franz had joined the Waffen-SS-Totenkopfstandarte Thüringen and at the end of 1939 was summoned to the Hitler's Chancellery and detailed for service as cook in the euthanasia institutes at Grafeneck, Hartheim, Sonnenstein and Brandenburg. As member of the 6th battalion he served at the Buchenwald concentration camp in 1941 and in the spring of 1942 was ordered to the General Government where he was posted to Belzec. He worked as a cook and trained the Ukrainian guards there before being given a new posting to Treblinka as Stangl's deputy. It did not take long before Franz made his mark at Treblinka, becoming one of the most dominant SS men in the camp. The prisoners saw him as one of the cruellest and most frightening figures in the camp. He was nicknamed 'Lalke' (doll in Yiddish) owing to his baby face. Often he would be seen riding on his horse touring the camp, visiting the work sites in the lower camp and the extermination area. When he was not roaming the camp he took part in the roll calls and meted out harsh punishments on the prisoners.

(**Above, right**) A portrait photograph of Alfred Forker. He was posted to Treblinka in 1942 and undertook guard duties in Camp II. His duties also included the sorting yard. (*H.E.A.R.T.*)

(**Opposite, above**) From left to right, SS-Unterscharführer Paul Bredow (Head of 'Barracks A', the clothing sorting barracks), SS-Unterscharführer Willi Mentz (assigned to Camp II in the summer of 1942 and then to Camp I as chief Landwirtschaftskommando (Agricultural Command), SS-Unterscharführer Max Moller (posted to Camp I in the 'undressing yard', and farming), and SS-Scharführer Josef Hirtreiter, nicknamed 'Sepp' by his comrades; he was appointed to Treblinka in October 1942 until October 1943. His main duties were in Camp II. (*H.E.A.R.T*)

(**Opposite, below**) A photograph taken probably in the late summer of 1942 showing Stangl and his deputy Franz at a doorway to the SS barracks. Stangl is wearing his familiar white tunic and holding an ox-hide whip. (*ARC*)

SS-Rottwachtmeister Willy Grossmann. His main duties were in Camp II and he received prisoners on the platform when deportations arrived. *(H.E.A.R.T.)*

Treblinka station. Stangl had ordered the construction of a fake railway station to fool the new arrivals into believing they had arrived at a genuine station to a transit camp. There were fake doors and windows, a fake Waiting Room, Information Telegraph Office, Station Manager, Rest Rooms, and many trees and beds of flowers. *(ARC)*

SS and Ukrainian guards pose for the camera outside the fake Treblinka station in the early spring of 1943. *(ARC)*

The camp zoo constructed near the Ukrainian barracks on the orders of Stangl in the early summer of 1943. Here the SS spent their leisure time sitting on wooden benches and tables relaxing and enjoying looking at the animals *(ARC)*

(**Above**) Barry the St. Bernard sitting for a photograph, probably taken by Kurt Franz. Barry had been trained by Franz to be particularly ferocious, and on his command he would attack Jews, biting at their bodies and sinking his teeth into the victim's genitals, occasionally ripping them off. *(H.E.A.R.T.)*

(**Opposite**) Two photographs showing SS-men using the excavators for the burial pits at Treblinka. Because of the huge flood of transports into the camp more prisoners were required to be selected for work detail to bury thousands of corpses. More burial pits were dug, sometimes by an excavator as seen here. The excavator had been brought over from Treblinka I and was used every day. It was built by Menk & Hambrock, a type 'Ma' produced between 1933 and 1944. These photos were taken by Stangl's deputy Kurt Franz. The photos were all found in his Treblinka album entitled 'Schone Zeiten' (Pleasant Times). *(ARC)*

Two photographs showing SS-men on the buckets of the excavator, probably in the first half of 1943. At least two types of excavators were used in Treblinka: bucket and cable. It was later realized that the bucket excavator was not very effective for digging burial pits. (ARC)

Chapter Three

Last Years

According to the chief statistician of the SS, Richard Korherr, who was responsible for compiling a progress report on the 'Final Solution', 2.7 million Jews were killed in 1942. The Operation Reinhard camps, notably Treblinka, Sobibor, Belzec, and the smaller camp of Majdanek, dominated the process.

In the first month of 1943 the war in Russia was not going well for the Nazis. Reverberations caused by the setbacks on the Eastern Front were increasingly felt at the Reinhard camps. The rolling stock for transporting victims to the death camps was desperately needed at the same time by the army to move troops and equipment.

German war production at the end of 1942 was suffering bottlenecks due to the shortage of labour. The destruction of the Jewish ghettos in Poland had a serious impact on industrial production there. The deportation of the Jews to Treblinka from the Warsaw ghetto for instance had halved textile production. The authorities responsible for overseeing production in the occupied territories proposed that they retain those Jews who were engaged in war production. Senior SS officials in the General Government had also become concerned; because the SS had employed considerable amounts of Jewish labour for their lucrative businesses. It was proposed that the fit Jews who had been left behind during the evacuation of the ghettos could be hired out to businesses for cash on a daily basis, returning to labour camps at night. The new policy meant that there would be fewer transports shipping 'cargo' to the extermination centres of the General Government.

In the meantime, however, shipments to the Reinhard camps were kept busy in early 1943 because of problems with the completion of the new gas chambers at Auschwitz. Adolf Eichmann had been eager to transfer Jewish transports for immediate liquidation to Auschwitz, but was now reluctantly forced to redirect trains to Treblinka and Sobibor. Belzec had ceased its killing activity before the end of 1942. The redirection of the shipments to the two remaining Reinhard camps were an administrative nightmare, but thanks to Eichmann's experience and careful planning he was able to undertake the deliveries without too much difficulty.

Between March and May 1943, deportations of Jews were once again on the increase for Sobibor and Treblinka. Auschwitz too reported it was running at full capacity and would soon become the largest killing centre in the Reich. However, the clearing of the ghettos in the General Government was virtually complete, and Treblinka and Sobibor were receiving the last deliveries by early summer 1943.

In October and November Treblinka was dismantled and closed down. On 20 November transport wagons 'Nos 22757, 22536, 70136, 139789' were shipped out to Sobibor. The end of Treblinka was the end of Operation Reinhard.

Auschwitz-Birkenau had now become the main death factory. It was from Hungary that the largest transports of Jews were sent to Auschwitz. By mid-May 1944, 3,300 Hungarians per day were arriving at the camp. By 28 May, it was reported, 184,049 Jews had arrived in Auschwitz in fifty-eight trains. Birkenau was gassing 8,000 Jews a day. The crematoria were operating at full capacity, and the incineration ditches were also being used day and night. The gassings and burnings carried on for days and weeks regardless of the deteriorating military situation. In just eight weeks Höss, the commandant, had masterminded the killing of more than 320,000 Hungarian Jews.

The Russians were now fighting on Polish soil east of Warsaw. On 6 September 1944 Himmler suddenly ordered the liquidation of Auschwitz and the destruction of all four crematoria including Bunkers I and II. All personal effects from the ware-houses, as well as building material and equipment, were to be transported back to the Reich. Half of the 150,000 prisoners held in Auschwitz, most of them Poles and Russians, were to be moved to concentration camps in the west. Höss was informed that Buchenwald, Bergen-Belsen, Dachau, Flossenbürg, Gross-Rosen, Mauthausen, Natzweiler, and Ravensbrück were to receive the Auschwitz prisoners. The sur-rounding sub-camps too were closed down and the workers there force-marched back to Germany to be used as slave labour. At Birkenau the Sonderkommando dismantled all the killing apparatus. The incineration ditches were cleared and levelled, and the pits which had been filled with the ash and crushed bones of murdered prisoners were emptied and covered with fresh turf and other plantation. Crema-torium I in the main camp was turned into an air-raid shelter and the chimney and holes in the ceiling into which the Zyklon B had been thrown were removed. All the furnaces of Crematoria I, II, III and IV were dismantled and usable parts transported to other camps. On the night of 17 January 58,000 prisoners were evacuated from Monowitz and the Auschwitz sub-camps. Very few were evacuated by train, most were forced into the snow and marched, often at night, towards Germany.

Jewish men, women and children disembark from a cattle cart and queue for selection. (*Auschwitz-Birkenau / USHMM*)

A photograph showing prisoners in the *Aufräumungskommando* (order commandos) sorting through a mound of personal belongings confiscated from the arriving transport of Jews in the summer of 1944. (*Auschwitz-Birkenau / USHMM*)

Another photograph showing *Aufräumungskommando* sorting through personal belongings. (*Auschwitz-Birkenau / USHMM*)

Prisoners in the *Aufräumungskommando* unload the confiscated property from a transport of Jews at a warehouse in Auschwitz-Birkenau.

Female Auschwitz inmates sort through a huge pile of shoes from the transport of Hungarian Jews.

Jewish men, women and children are being loaded onto a cattle car bound to a fait that can only be imagined.

Jews being loaded onto a train. By the summer of 1943, clearing of the ghettos in the General Government was virtually complete, and both Treblinka and Sobibor were receiving the last deliveries. Over the next few months it saw the Germans liquidating the last ghettos in Poland at a tremendous rate. Their inhabitants were either exterminated or deported to the labour camps.

An aerial view of Belzec in 1940.

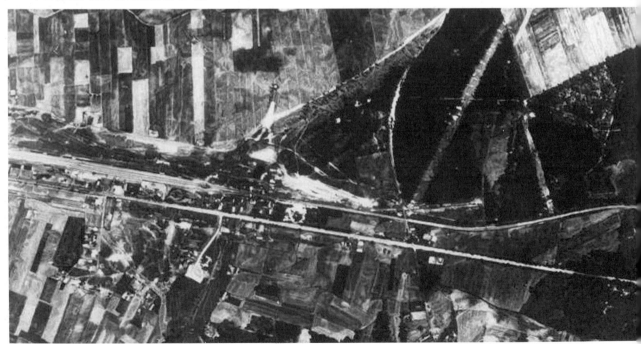

An aerial view of Belzec in 1944. Note that lots of earth has been moved after the camp was dismantled, compared with the previous Belzec camp photo.

An aerial photo of the Sobibor area of Poland showing the camp and its immediate surroundings.

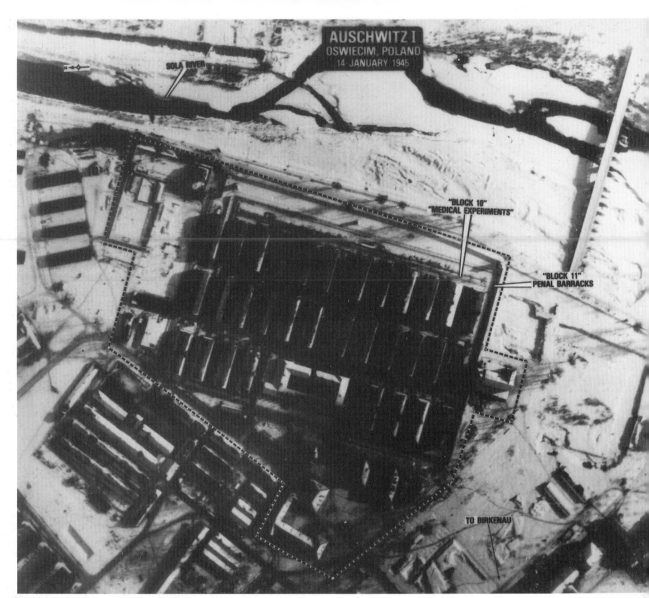

AUSCHWITZ I
OSWIECIM, POLAND
14 JANUARY 1945

SOLA RIVER

"BLOCK 10"
"MEDICAL EXPERIMENTS"

"BLOCK 11"
PENAL BARRACKS

TO BIRKENAU

(**Above**) An Allied aerial reconnaissance photograph taken on 14 January 1945 showing the main camp Auschwitz I. The commandant of Auschwitz, Rudolf Höss', family residence sits at the end of the block barracks nearest to the road overlooking the Sola River. (*Auschwitz-Birkenau Museum*)

(**Opposite, above**) An Allied aerial reconnaissance photograph taken on 13 September 1944 showing Auschwitz-Birkenau, also known as Auschwitz II. The photograph clearly identifies all the camp's crematoria, transport and probable prisoners or camp personnel. The image also shows the railway line travelling through to Crematoria II and III. However, because of restrictions on vital materials due to the war this never reached the killing facilities. Those unloaded would have to walk the short distance to their death instead. (*Auschwitz-Birkenau Museum*)

(**Opposite, below**) An aerial photograph of the remains of the Treblinka camp taken in September 1944, 11 months after the dismantling of the camp, and after attempts at disguising the site as a farm. (*NARA*)

BIRKENAU EXTERMINATION CAMP
OSWIECIM, POLAND
13 SEPTEMBER 1944

N

GAS CHAMBERS II & III

GAS CHAMBERS IV & V

WOMEN'S CAMP

TRANSPORTS

PRISONERS

PROBABLE PRISONERS

PRISONERS

ENLARGED FROM THE ORIGINAL NEGATIVE AND
CAPTIONED IN 1978 BY THE CIA

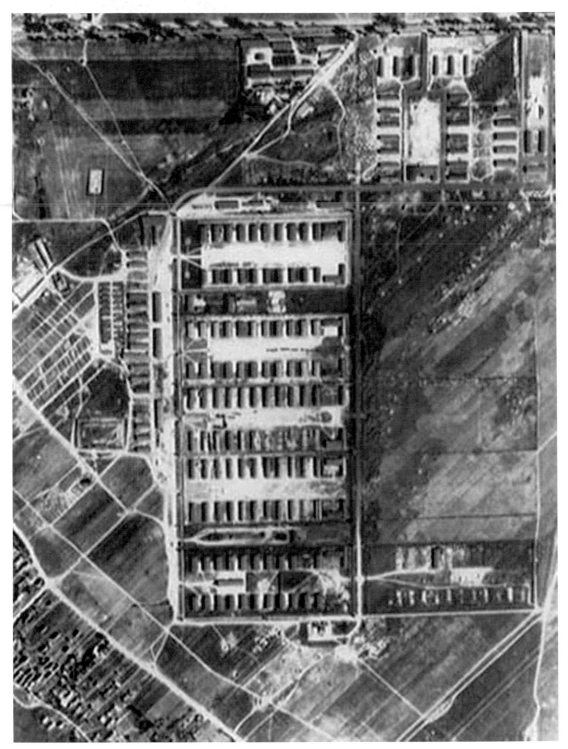

An aerial view of Majdanek and Lublin suburbs.

An aerial view of the grounds at Chełmno.

The Main Polish Death Camps

Camp	Function	Location	Est.	Evacuated	Liberated	Est. No. Murdered
Chełmno	Extermination	Chełmno, Poland	7 Dec 1941 to 23 June 1944	Closed March 1943 (but reopened); liquidated July 1944	320,000	
Majdanek	Concentration Extermination	Lublin, Poland	16 Feb 1943	July 1944	24 July 1944 by Soviets	360,000
Auschwitz	Concentration Extermination	Oswiecim (near Krakow)	26 May 1940	18 Jan 1945	27 Jan 1945 by Soviets	1,100,000
Treblinka	Extermination	near Warsaw	23 July 1942	Revolt on 2 April 1943; liquidated by SS, April 1943		800,000
Sobibor	Extermination	near Lublin	March 1942	Revolt on 14 October 1943; liquidated October 1943	Summer 1944 by Soviets	250,000
Belzec	Extermination	Belzec, Poland	17 March 1942	Liquidated by Nazis, December 1942		600,000

Notes

Notes

Notes

Notes

Notes